The Family Album

The Family Album

PHOTOGRAPHS OF THE 1890s & 1900s BY GILBERT WIGHT TILTON & FRED W. RECORD

Assembled by Mark Silber

David R. Godine

DAVID R. GODINE   PUBLISHER
Boston, Massachusetts

Copyright © 1973 by Mark Silber

LCC 73-75835
ISBN 0-87923-069-x

TO

GILBERT WIGHT TILTON

AND

FRED W. RECORD

FOREWORD

BY WESTON J. NAEF

TWO POINTS REGARDING the photographs in this book should be made clear at the outset. They are the work of talented amateur photographers, and they are primarily snapshots. The words 'amateur' and 'snapshots' are most critical, and more should be said about both.

From the earliest moments of photography the work of amateurs has possessed a vitality and personal expressiveness lacking in much professional work. The first amateurs in the history of the medium were Scottish country gentlemen who practiced W. F. Talbot's new calotype process during the 1840s and 1850s. We find their work in family albums from the period just as we would encounter photographs by amateurs in albums today. The subjects are generally single portraits, a family group, a view of the house, or a look down the property. These photographs are possessed of an eerie stillness caused by the fact that the materials were relatively insensitive to light and therefore required very long exposures, sometimes of ten or fifteen minutes, which meant that only absolutely still subjects would come out well. As a result the portraits are very posed and the subjects seldom ever caught off guard. Nevertheless these calotypes generally are more revealing than the contemporary daguerreotypes, a more perfect but highly formal kind of photograph generally made by professional photographers rather than amateurs.

One of the characteristics shared by amateur photographers then and now is less concern for the technical particulars of how and why an image is produced than for the overall communicative power of the image itself. This is particularly the case with a photographer like Julia Margaret Cameron, active a generation after Talbot's contemporaries, who did not take up the medium until middle age. She barely learned how to coat the glass plate with the light-sensitive wet collodion used to make the negative, and was so little concerned with darkroom procedures that her negatives often had distracting spots and many of her prints faded needlessly. In spite of the arduous process of preparing each plate just before exposure and developing it immediately afterwards, she acted like any amateur of today in taking pictures of the friends and relatives nearest to her. It is true that some of her friends happened to be celebrities like the poet Tennyson and the scientist Herschel; however, she did not seek out celebrities as did professional portrait photographers. While the medium still required sitters to remain motionless, Cameron's photographs are, in their subject matter, essentially snapshots.

Though amateurs practiced the medium of photography even when it was complicated and cumbersome, as technological advances made things simpler their numbers increased and the snapshot as we think of it gradually emerged. The key steps in this process of development were the invention of the dry plate and along with it emulsions sufficiently light sensitive to permit shutter speeds fast enough to stop motion, a position generally arrived at by the mid-1870s. By the early 1880s easily portable box-type cameras with complicated hanging devices for the glass plates made the camera even more versatile. Finally the introduction of flexible film made possible George Eastman's *Kodak* box camera and brought photography to a state not greatly different from its state today.

The final step in democratizing photography was the service offered by the Kodak company of allowing the photographer to send his camera with the film inside to the factory for developing and printing. George Eastman's slogan 'You press the button, we do the rest' heralded the snapshot era.

To call the photographers in this book snapshooters in spite of the seriousness with which they took their craft is not to belittle their accomplishment, since the snapshot might very well be the most important form of visual communication between generations of ordinary men ever to have existed. It is in the capacity to capture the fleeting moment that turn-of-the-century amateur photographers differed from their antecedents, since both the early calotypists and the workers in collodion like Julia Margaret Cameron could photograph only motionless subjects, with a consequent lack of animation in their poses.

All photographs, whether posed or animated, made it possible for more people than ever before to know what their ancestors looked like. The snapshot, though, revealed not only the ancestor's image, but the person engaged in those activities that helped to describe a manner of casual response, as well as his enthusiasms and other surface cues of personality.

The snapshot is, further, a slice through time that reveals many details of an environment. With a portable camera that could operate even with very little light it was possible for every background to be different, a point easily forgotten in the present age of miniature cameras, but very important when one considers the prevalence of standardized backgrounds before 1880. The snapshot very often tells us as much about the subject through accurate rendering of surrounding details as it does in portraying bodily features.

The importance of extraneous details is easy to underestimate until we imagine how much narrative would be needed to describe in words every detail represented in the average snapshot – such items as costume, decorative accessories, architecture, the nature and covering of wall surfaces (whether freshly enameled porches, weatherbeaten clapboards, or the complexity of pattern laid upon pattern in the wallpaper), rugs, and the upholstery common in the Victorian interior. It would take an awesome memory and deft verbal skills to pass all these details on from one generation to the next through oral or written history. As a result of the snapshot we probably know more about our immediate ancestors than any previous generation.

The snapshot is in many ways a symbolic form of communication relatively independent of the literal identification of the events portrayed. This is nowhere more evident than in the dialogue that accompanies these photographs. Names, places, and specific events are often not remembered, yet the photographs retain meaning not only for the descendants, but also for us, the unrelated, objective observers. The reasons why an anonymous family album has powerful meaning are not easy to give. The answer in part is that the snapshot is a new form of history, one based on the symbols of every man's life in the early twentieth century – his residence and possessions, his animals, his entertainment, his manner of showing affection – objects, activities, and states of mind of ordinary people that went largely unrecorded before the amateur and his camera.

METROPOLITAN MUSEUM OF ART
November 1972

INTRODUCTION

BY MARK SILBER

THE PHOTOGRAPHS that follow were taken at the turn of the century by Gilbert 'Burt' Tilton and Fred W. Record. The two were friends and business partners in the small town of Buckfield, Maine. They were not artists or photographers; rather, they were representative of the many amateurs of that period who were delving for the first time into the brand-new hobby of photography. But at the same time they succeeded in achieving high technical quality and creative excellence.

Tilton and Record took pictures for only a few years during their late teens and early twenties. They had been friends from childhood and remained constant companions until their deaths in the 1960s. Together they ran a carriage shop, then a bicycle shop; and with the advent of the automobile they started the first garage in town.

The speakers in the dialogue accompanying the photos are Tilton's and Record's nearest living relatives. Gilbert Tilton is the son of Burt Tilton. Henry Bridgham is the nephew of Fred Record. The interview with them was conducted in the late summer and early fall of 1972 in their homes. Tilton's son, in his fifties, is the owner of a Buckfield grocery store. Henry Bridgham, who was brought up by Record, is a fire warden for the state of Maine.

Buckfield is located in Oxford County, a hilly rural area of southwestern Maine. It has a population of nearly 1500, about the same as that of seventy years ago. Some of the residents are direct descendants of the Mayflower's Plymouth settlers. In fact, Buckfield was settled largely by Massachusetts colonists who ventured northward, back when Maine was part of that state, to receive their share of the free hundred acres given away by the Commonwealth.

By Tilton's and Record's time, Buckfield was bustling with activity. Like many small New England communities, the town during the nineteenth century had experienced a sharp transition from an agricultural to a more industrial economy. At the turn of the century, Buckfield was a center for the manufacture of brushes, boots and shoes, sleds, snow shovels, boxes, and toothpicks. When Tilton and Record were coming of age, new factories were still being built, the issues of the day were being publicly debated by the newly formed Buckfield literary club, and the town had had a native son appointed Secretary of the Navy. John D. Long of Buckfield was running the Great White Fleet that defeated the Spanish in Cuba and the Philippines.

Things are quieter today. Very few of the industries of the late nineteenth century have survived. Most of Buckfield's modern-day residents are self employed in trades or light farming, work out of town in factories or offices, or else are involved in the apple growing industry. Today, the two local stores, a Baptist church, and the public schools are the centers of the town's social life.

It was at Tilton's grocery store that a discussion of old photographs arose. At the time I had just finished my book *Rural Maine*. The photographing and the publication of this book by a newcomer to Buckfield had been a matter of some public attention. Gilbert Tilton mentioned that he had a few photographs that his father had taken. He brought out a small album of faded brown snapshots that, by the appearance of the costumes, I judged to have been taken in the early part of this century. What was particularly exciting was the general liveliness of these images. Seldom had I seen such a fluid treatment of people or such variety of perception and simultaneous lack of stiffness.

I viewed the photographs with excitement, hoping that the negatives had survived, though I doubted that they could have been saved in the shuffle of years. To my surprise we found them still stored in boxes in Tilton's barn. I examined them and discovered that, with a few exceptions, they were salvageable. Many were interleaved with cut newspaper strips. Silver crystallization was present, some negatives were chipped and the emulsion cracked, but the images had remained. My excitement grew when another batch was contributed by Henry Bridgham. His negatives, like Tilton's, were still in the original boxes. The expiration dates read: 'Develop before 1901.'

The camera Burt Tilton and Fred Record used was the Cyclone SR, made by the Western Camera Manufacturing Company of New York and Chicago, which was later bought out by the burgeoning Eastman Kodak Company. The Cyclone took 4×5 inch glass plates. The camera and negative carriers, as well as the red homemade safety lamp, are still in existence.

Some plates I found were made by the Stanley Dry Plate Company in Newton, Massachusetts. Other boxes of negatives were made by the Standard Dry Plate Company in Rochester, N.Y. and the Cramer Dry Plate Works in St. Louis, Mo. Cramer plates were called 'Non-Halation Plates' and were manufactured under Roche's patents. Locally, some of these boxes were distributed by Wilfred Bowler of Bethel, Maine. Bowler had a photography studio and probably was involved, at least peripherally, with the instruction given to Record and Tilton. A box similar to those mentioned had contained one gross of 4×5 Sensitized Albuma Paper, manufactured by the New Jersey Aristotype Company in Nepera Park, N.Y. One gross was priced at $1.25. These were the materials used by the two photographers of the Buckfield social life.

Although the late 1890s and early 1900s witnessed great popularization of the new nitrocellulose 'film' as the base for the light sensitive emulsion, many photographers like Tilton and Record

13 ꧁

kept on using glass plates. Their technique was doubtless influenced by the non-availability of the new materials as well as the slow penetration of the information into the rural areas.

Remote as it was, Buckfield was part of a United States burning with the excitement of the last quarter of the nineteenth century. It was a time of industrial growth, a revolutionary period that saw the inventions of the telephone, electric light, talking machine, and gasoline engine. New petroleum, chemical, manufacturing, and transportation industries were springing up. At the same time the country was witnessing the 'reconstruction' of the South, the exploration and expansion of the West, and wars with Spain in Cuba and the Philippines. The countries of the Far East were beginning to attract attention. There was much to be enthusiastic about and to wonder at. All this influenced the middle class American life and family.

The development and growth of photography also had a significant influence on the individual. With the daguerrotype appeared a new era in communication and representation. However, photography by its sheer complexity excluded most non-professionals. The wet plate (collodion) method, for example, required a darkroom on the spot. Amateurs had to be wealthy enough to afford the time required and the expense of the needed equipment. With gradual refinements the medium slowly grew more popular. At first only a very few people could afford photos of themselves. A long gap occurred between the appearance of the first photographs and the time when the ambrotype and the wet collodian lowered the price of image production. Prints came to be made on paper. Most of the prints I have seen in Buckfield that survived from Tilton's and Record's time were studio images produced on paper or tin.

Forty years before Tilton and Record photographed, the *carte de visite* (a 2½ × 4 inch photo mounted on cardboard) brought studio photography to the zenith of its popularity. In this period appeared the first family albums. At first albums were filled with the *cartes de visite.* Mass produced in studios in New York and Washington, the images at one point reached a price as low as twenty-five for a dollar. These cards were traded among friends, relations, neighbors, and other associates. Stiff, small, and awkward, they were anything but epitomes of visual freedom; nevertheless, they filled the albums manufactured by Anthony's and Frederick's, the photographic studios and suppliers of New York.

Later, a larger image area appeared to restimulate the photographic business. A cabinet size of approximately 4 × 5 inches allowed for better picture quality. The albums increased in size, and their prices ranged between $1.50 and $45.00. The cabinet size spurred the development of more complicated backgrounds in the studios and allowed better enlargements, up to 'imperial' and life sizes. These very expensive prints cost from $500 to $700 apiece.

Although the introduction of the family album in the United States can be traced to the early 1860s, few if any of the earliest ones contained photographs by amateurs or members of the family. But this situation changed dramatically in the late 1870s when the dry photographic plate was introduced. The dry plate for the first time allowed the photographer to discard the 'portable' darkroom and venture out on picture-taking expeditions. It also brought an important new standardization to photography; for the first time it was possible to have a batch of gelatine emulsion plates with approximately the same overall sensitivity to light. Doing away with the wet process meant that more people were able to afford the equipment and the time, and more were able to participate in the growing hobby of photography.

Now the family was able to make an image anywhere, instan-

15 ෨ᘐ

taneously, with any one of a number of the cameras that flooded the market. The potentialities of photography were widened. The freedom from the immediate need for a darkroom created possibilities for a new imagery. The ripened emulsion of the dry plate increased flexibility. This atmosphere allowed for the growth of photographers like Tilton and Record: the family album, for the first time, was being filled by the documents of everyday life. The medium prospered by creating the home photographer, the documentor of his own life and times.

This is what Tilton and Record accomplished *par excellence*. The record they left is a family album. Its importance lies in their individualistic interpretation of their lives, through the candid reportage of leisure activities. What we learn about the people of that time in the interviews that follow is merely the confirmation of what we see in the photographs. The photos reflect a freedom of movement, gaiety, and life, and although they are social documents of the time, they do not attempt to portray a social stratum other than the photographers' own. Theirs is not a cerebral treatment of an era. It is totally unlike the street work of John Thompson and Paul Martin in England, or Riis, Genthe, and Hine in the United States. The social document is generally associated with the urban condition or with the exploration of an exotic land and its people. By contrast, the portrayal here is the result of neither intellectual treatment, artistic considerations, nor political motivation. Nevertheless, this document has historical merit and artistic value.

It is a record of New England country life, created to preserve memories for those involved, memories of the excitement and joys of careless youth. For the subjects and the photographers, youth was inexorably replaced by the cares and responsibilities of adulthood. The camera was put away. The momentary flair of activity, the spirit of instantaneous discovery, the delight of youth, was recorded and forgotten.

❧ 16

The Family Album

That's my dad.

Like a thunderbird in a snow.

That's right. They jump up in the air and spread-eagle their arms and legs and someone snapped a picture of him no doubt.

Backdrop. ... It must have been wintertime. I can't imagine how he got that white effect, can you?

Time exposure? What do you think – it's snow on the ground with a white sky?

He's laying on the snowbank, I think. And I guess they did it upside down to make him right side up.

19 ✇

That's typical old Maine, all right. Those are white leghorns.

You can remember just such places.

Yep, typical.

Right. One hundred percent. I feel comfortable with that picture. I can identify with that.

That's about thirty hens there and that's about what they would have –

Thirty to fifty hens, a couple of cows, and a few pigs and a horse and raise a little garden. Get by all right.

One thing they didn't have: they didn't have taxes or they couldn't have done it. Probably the tax on that building for a year was about twelve dollars.

I think that's probably Thomas. If it's anybody.

Well, I go along with that.

He's posing with his older brother's bicycle.

That was about the time of the first bicycle craze.

You know, I have some pictures like that, I'm pretty sure. Fred's on a bicycle like that.

Downcast handles there, down under your knees. The same way they affect them now.

23 ❧

Oh yes, here we go. That's Dot. Dressed up in the clothes of their men, I guess.

You think that's Sadie Maxim? That's Dot.

This is Sadie. I'd say dressed up in their husbands' clothes.

They probably were married by that time. That's at the pond all right. Hm, they are pretty good lookers. Really – weren't they? Hair right underneath their hats.

They probably spent some time ...

Oh yeah, they probably put in hours at that.

Didn't spare any details.

Nope, everything was there, pipe and all. Women might do that today, possibly. Gee, not too many years ago some guy dressed up in those women's things, posed as a patient in a doctor's office and just barely got by. ...

27 ❧

I think this building where the picture was taken is presently being used as a restaurant, right here in Buckfield. It's in the back room of that building.

What used to be the battery room, probably.

That's what they called it then. Of course, previous to then, they repaired wagons. You see that wagon wheel in there.

I think I enjoyed discovering this picture 'bout as much as any.

But who it is I don't know.

Could've been a wandering minstrel very easily. There were some. I can remember genuine medicine shows being here in town with the Indians and the fire water and the whole works.

Oh, now I remember his name – Dr. Welby.

Yeah, with the snake oil – 'Don't forget the snake oil for the rheumatism.' Yeah, yeah.

This fellow was alone. He wasn't part of any show; just a wandering minstrel, a blind person: his eyes look kind of strange there in the picture. He might've been a blind musician going around trying to play for coins or whatever anyone would give him.

A place to sleep and something to eat.

Rebecca at the well. Undoubtedly a spoof. But that's who it is: Rebecca L. Record, and the well, and the receptacle. That almost has to be a posed idea. Somebody thought that up.

But I think they'd thought it up and gone out there to have their picture taken.

That was just a way of life just the same in spite of it. You went out and got your water at the well and you probably used that little can or whatever that is. You carried it into the house.

You known that in the city of Boston in 1837 you weren't allowed to take a bath in a bathtub without orders from the doctor.

No, really?

One hundred percent true. I just read letters ... I think it's true. I read it in a book today. Kind of struck me funny. Well, the bathtub was a new thing at that time. They weren't sure anybody should take a hot bath. They didn't know what kind of effect it would have on the human body. The bathtub is a relatively recent invention.

Well, do you figure that was Nat Morill?

It's in front of Nat Morill's barn.

He used to have bulls. He's got one on a staff there. Leading stick, isn't it? Stick right through his nose so the bull can't get too close. You hold that stick out, you see, and he can't reach you.

Safety measure, I guess.

Of course that's one of the most dangerous animals in the world — the domestic bull. Makes a tiger look like a pussy cat.

That barn has been torn down within the last year.

Yep, right.

Well that's Rebecca L. and I think that's Guy Gardner in the middle. Who the other is I don't know.

He was a druggist up to Dixfield, right? He run a drugstore up in Dixfield for years and years. I'd suppose he might have been a year or two younger than the rest. He's always standing there with a broom over his shoulder, so I think he was the dog-rubber of the outfit. The one who did the dirty chores like sweeping out and so forth. You'd always see pictures of him there with a broom over his shoulder hanging out like it was a gun.

That's Rebecca L. on the chaise lounge there. I believe it's up to Tilton's there. I believe as though I recognize the chairs.

Nope, those chairs weren't up to Tilton's, where these pictures were taken. The chairs that I have are similar to these. They came from my grandmother's home. They weren't up in our home until the nineteen twenties or thirties, so they couldn't have been the same ones.

I just wish we knew some way. There's no way we're ever gonna know. Nobody's gonna know, ever.

The sheep herding business wasn't big at that time.

I'd like to argue that. Some old-timers told me that they had sheep drives where they would run them through town. When the sheep are crossing the bridge and leaving the town going toward Turner and the first of the group of sheep are on that bridge, the back end of the group of sheep would be on the bridge to the village. So that is quite a lot of sheep to fill the road between the two bridges.

I would say it was up at Damon's.

Would Gardner hill show from this angle?

No, you would be looking past the barn. You would be missing Gardner Hill, which would be further off to the right there.

Now they only have a few sheep here and there.

This has to be the bicycle shop.

But not the one in Buckfield.

I guess it's the old horse there for repairs. What would you say, Tilton? Down-curved handlebars there. No foot brakes at that time. If you wanted to stop, you'd just push backwards. That didn't always use to work. But if that didn't work, I'd just take my shoe and put it back against the rear wheel. It'd brake on the rear wheel.

I usually ran into a tree.

43 ❦

Now that one we know about. That house is gone. The river is still there. There—you name those off, Tilton.

Left to right, George Brown, Babe Wood, and Will Record. They're sawing the ice on Nezinscot River just about where the former railroad bridge was.

That was a mill pond there. You could saw ice there where now it's just a rapids. There was a dam right under the railroad bridge. That went out with the high waters. Probably in 1936, wasn't it?

I fished up there many hours at a time before it went. It was an unusual dam. The other dams were on the river below the village and they were of granite. This one was made of logs that were crisscrossed and notched and staked.

Yeah, that's gone. That's departed.

Dot and Sadie having a little joyous spring dance there. I'd like to know where that place is. One thing I can tell you for sure. That's a Franklin stove. It says so right on the bottom.

I'd say that would be the usual bunch. That looks like Maud.

Sure that's Maud, sure.

Sure, that must've been her husband: Henry T. P. Bates.

Now what time did he live? Did he ... did he ... die?

He died quite young so they weren't married too long. I never saw him. I'm named for him, but the only picture of him that I saw was—oh I don't know, I don't believe that could be him. This man has a walrus mustache and looks quite old, so I assume he's quite a lot older than Maud. So that evidently wasn't H. T. P. Bates.

That's Maud. She used to bicycle from Massachusetts to Maine, summers, even when she got to be quite an older lady, didn't she Bridgham?

Ah-yeah, she was eighty some when she used to come up. ...

What—by bicycle?

And she was over ninety when she climbed the Streaked Mountain on foot.

Oh, I didn't know that.

Well, she died ten years ago, in her nineties. I imagine it wasn't more than ten years ago.

Apparently she was a school teacher for many years ... and ... I guess you could figure it out.

She weighed only ninety pounds.

She was even smaller than Rebecca L.

Never married—only that first time, and she made her way after that as a teacher in Massachusetts. She died in Dedham. She was here off and on. She might come up here a couple of weeks maybe in the summer.

She used to come up. Of course, 'twas before the traffic got quite as severe as it is now. I don't know how long it took her, but I would say probably a week. I think she ought to make it easy in a week. She had one of the first of the bicycles we saw around here with the different speeds. She used the Raleigh. She was very much the booster of the Raleigh machine. That was about the first one that came from England. She's the one on the right.

That might be Guy Gardner, but I don't think he was that tall. He had a derby hat on usually. I would suppose these people were high society as high society went in the town. I don't mean high society as you mean it, but I mean people who had a few more things than the average. Quite a lot of people were working in the woods, doing hard heavy manual labor. And these people were a little bit better off.

Will Warren ran a harness shop and was the proprietor of the hotel.

There were two. On High Street that wasn't a hotel, I don't think. That was part of my relations' doctor's establishment there.

The big building up in the vee of the road. That's where the celebrated murder took place.

In the Bridgham family we had a really good murder that took place up there in that house. One Bridgham tried to brain another with a chair, and the first Bridgham went out of the room and came back with a .44 Smith and Wesson American and laid him 'mongst the sweet peas right there on the kitchen floor.

Was he caught?

Sure he was caught. They had a trial. And they called it justifiable homicide. Fellow tried to conk him on the head with a chair. You would kill a man who did that, wouldn't you?

That was after the Civil War, 'cause that was Tom Bridgham. He came back. Evidently he was some kind of an officer in the Civil War—Union side, I dare say. Henry's grandfather was in the Civil War and in the Union forces, but when he came home and started raising his family he named a lot of boys after General Lee. Your uncle was Robert T. Lee Bridgham.

Evidently old Bill thought quite a lot of Lee's tactics.

After the war was over they had the feeling that all this animosity was pretty nearly wasted away, very quickly. And the northern troops thought a lot of Lee, and the southern troops probably . . . well, losers wouldn't be apt to be quite so magnanimous.

And Grover Cleveland Bridgham was my father, you see.

There—I recognize it. That's the picture that's in my back room there. But as to who that is, I haven't got the foggiest ...

Well, that would be Fred's mother.

Fred played the violin. He never claimed he could, but I guess he really could play it fairly well. He considered himself a rather poor violin player— in fact he wouldn't play towards the end. But I did hear him. What little I know of music, I thought he was a good violinist.

You know, I asked him one time, if they had a minstrel show or local talent singing or any playing, if he wouldn't go. But he wouldn't. I asked my father why Fred wouldn't go, and he said he couldn't stand it. He couldn't stand to hear any music played and not have it played as it should be. So he must have had a tremendous ear for music ...

He did.

... if it bothered him so much. I mean, see, he could pick out the stuff right off the radio. He fooled with radios a lot. But he claimed they weren't right—some of the pieces which were played, which weren't too many when radio first came around. There was about three songs and that was it. He considered it terrible stuff.

I remember being up here listening to the radio and if they were playing some music, some really good music, he'd turn it way down so he could just barely hear. He'd sit right there and he wouldn't turn up the volume. He would play it very low.

Well, you see, he wouldn't want to hear any noise. In those times your transmission of sound was such that if you had it high, it was distorted. Your radio speakers and earphones weren't so good. He always claimed that earphones was way ahead of a speaker. Said you got truer musical notes and stuff through the headphone than you did through the speaker any day. That was back when they started out.

Do you know where that was taken, Tilton?

North Pond camp — I'm positively sure of that.

That's the usual bunch.

They used to go on haystack rides. Dot did ride a horse some, I know, but I think probably they had wagons. When they went up to the lake country, I'd imagine they had a hayrack or a wagon — something to lug their supplies up. They'd get some farmer around there to transport them back and forth, if they didn't walk. Of course, it wouldn't have been a very severe walk from here either — not at that age.

That's James E. Warren on the right. The others I don't know.

58

That's Gilbert.

Yeah, that's my Dad. That's in the wintertime — he was firing a gun and he took the picture at the same time he fired and he got the smoke from the black powder.

That's probably that old gun that he owns. An old double gun. Don't it look like it to you?

It looks like the old Parker.

Oh yes, he was firing black powder then anyway.

That's the double barrel Parker. My father had a bird dog to go hunting with. And he was a good dog. He used to do that type of hunting. Never deer hunting, never that I know of.

Would have, but there wasn't any deer around here at that time. There was too many farms and they would cut the timber all off; there were just wood lots and that was no habitat for deer. As I was a young fellow, it was a rare, rare thing to see a deer. And as it kept growing up, the deer came in around the edges, and as they cut off, the deer worked the cut-offs. So that's what they had to have to survive. They can't exist in a grassland and they can't exist in a forest that is large. You've got to have your cuttings so that they can get their boughs that comes out.

That's a birthday party at Dr. Arthur Cole's home.

Who's the one with the dust cap?

That's either Helen or Margaret Shaw.

Oh yeah. I knew I've seen her. It was either Helen's birthday, or Arthur's birthday, or Sadie's birthday.

Well, that was before my time.

That's Dr. DeCosta. Evidently some lodge he belonged to. What might it be, Tilton?

Oh, Masonic, I'd reckon. Or Knight Templars, I think. My uncle had the same type of picture, the same plumed hat.

That's Fred W. Record going fishing with a derby hat on. That has to be up to the pond. He's joining up the old rod, getting ready to head out ... either that or he's getting ready to go home — either one or the other.

That top coat had a fur collar on it.

Can you imagine anybody going fishing in that kind of an outfit? I'd think he'd be afraid of getting it torn or slimed up or something.

That's a Sunday afternoon. It had to be.

This could very well have been taken in 1898. The only thing I can think of is that that young fellow there must be Joe Withington. He run the Withington Mills down there, the brush factory. I can't think of any reason why they're holding the poster up. They might've been strong Dewey supporters. Chances are that it was something to do with the war—celebrating the end of it maybe. I assume at that time they hung up posters of the famous men.

That's Rebecca L. Record and that's a later picture. I can remember when she looked exactly like that. I bet she was dressed for some local show.
She was always interested in any local plays. She was in drama or the so-called minstrel shows. Played Santa Claus at Christmastime for years and years.

71 ❧

That's supposed to be Bill Coffrin and his wife.

The sled is very unusual. This is taken in front of the present bank building, right here in Buckfield.

Them little runners are just made of common crooked trees, they smoothed them down a little, probably with an axe.

Tremendously big woman. It wouldn't seem that this sleigh-type thing would support that weight.

That's a pretty good bunch. No question of that. The only one I actually know there is Rebecca L.—Dot Record. And I'm pretty sure that sitting beside her is my father. He looks a great deal like I looked when I was his age. He was less than fifty when he died. Probably around forty.

Henry's mother and father both died with the flu about World War One.

It really killed you in those days. It was a virulent breed of flu and they didn't know what to do with it. I was born in 1917. They died, I would say, in the middle of winter in 1919. I was about a year and a half then.

77 ～

It makes me wheeze up to see those mattresses. You know I used to go up there by the way ...

Yeah, corn husk mattresses.

... and be dusty and I had asthma. I couldn't lay down on it.

Those are pretty dusty mattresses too. They probably never was taken out and beaten or anything like that to get the dust out of them. Then the natural dust that's in the air, of course — mattresses lay around and get all covered with dust. Gilbert could hit the mattress and after doing that he would be all out.

Sit up all night and couldn't sleep.

Or else he would be there snoring. He would be just 'bout living. We didn't consider it to be anything at the time, or people that was with him, but now I can see where he must've suffered more or less.

The only way I could breathe would be to lean over a chair; then sometimes take adrenalin to get my breath. Yes ... And then all of a sudden ...

It got better.

... it disappeared.

He can smoke.

That didn't bother me. It wasn't that, it had nothing to do, apparently, with smoking.

He used to smoke. What were those things you used to smoke?

Colberts.

Yeah! For asthma you smoked a cigarette as medicine.

Took belladonna ... and what was the other one? Used to take adrenalin. Used to take hypos with adrenalin and belladonna.

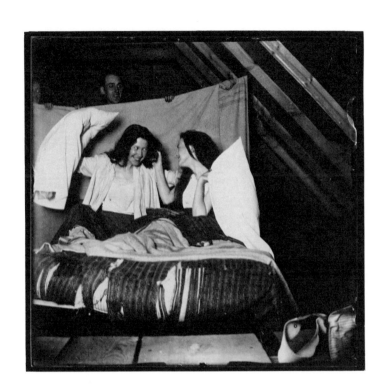

That's Will Allen's boat, isn't it? I don't think Rebecca rowed very well. That is, I can remember when she rowed for me. They weren't very good, the girls, but they would get in there and horse around, try to be rowing to get their picture taken.

Big deal!

Yes, yes. I think that's what it was. I doubt if she could row the boat across the North Pond in a week.

They look like Bridghams to me. They're ...

Ha ha ha!

They're nice looking boys and they're well dressed....

Ha ha ha — pardon me for laughing.

I would imagine there was some connection with one of the families there. otherwise they wouldn't waste film on just strangers, would they?

I'm pretty sure they are Bridghams. They are such fine looking young boys.

Ha ha ha!

That's the banana deal. Those are undoubtedly red bananas.
You don't know how many times I tried to get some red bananas
downtown. But I haven't yet. I've got the food manager so that now
when I mention the red bananas, he says, 'You're going to get the
red ones sometime.'

Gilbert's father is there and Rebecca L. is there. I don't know the gentle-man with the mustache, do you Gilbert? Big nose, unless it's Ellie Warren. Which I almost think it is. That time he had a mustache.

You look at it through here and I think it's Fred.

Could be, could be.

You notice their shirts were all matched. They had four shirts on, and they were all striped. Striped shirts, ha.

Now you think it's Fred?

I'm sure it is. Look at it through the glass.

Don't you think there is a mustache mixed up in there?

I don't think so, Bridgham.

That nose looks pretty big.

Well, you're looking down on it from a little different angle than you usually do. This I'm sure of. My father enjoyed doing carpenter work. I think he helped move the camp. He'd make repairs. My uncle built a camp up by Labrador Pond. My father was up there all the time while they were building it, and then after it was built he never went near it again. I mean, he was just interested in doing the work and building it, and afterward he ... he ... his interest just wasn't there.

That's not Fred, that's Ellie Warren. You look at it again.

I still think it's Fred.

How're you going to make that nose on Fred?

Well, I could be wrong.

Well, maybe what I'm seeing there as nose may be part of a tree, I don't know.

Ha ha ha. I think it's my father on the left.

Your father on the left?

Well, that's Fred on the ground there. I thought you were talking about the other one.

89 ⤜

That steamboat would be the Owassa, down on the river between Buckfield and Turner. They had it down there before they had it up to North Pond. They used to go to Turner Village with it.

They never did get down to Chaser's Mills with it, did they?

Oh sure. The dam was in then. You could go to Turner, and the best travelin' route would be to Chaser's Mills down.

You know, I've got that newspaper clipping, and it said they couldn't get down within sight of Chaser's Mills.

I fail to see why.

Well, I don't. It said in the newspaper clipping.

You couldn't believe the press then anymore than you can now. That 'butment is still there—the old bridge—but you couldn't even drive a boat down past it. If you go down the middle of the river you would hit that old 'butment where the old bridge is gone. But there is plenty of room to get around it. Tilton's father built the boat and I guess Fred built the engine.

I think Fred took his plans from the Stanley Steamer, didn't he? The thing looked very similar to it.

They had to get an inspector up from Portland before they could take any passengers out on the boat. I've got it somewhere where they inspected the boat and found it satisfactory to use for carrying passengers. And that was in 1900 and something.

Henry and I raised that boat. Found it sunk and raised it. And I've got the tiller out of it. I think some kids were responsible for the sinking.

Well, it might have been they had a hole in the bottom of it—you know, a drain, and there was rocks enough in it to sink it when we pulled it up. So I assume what they did is more or less filled it up full of rocks and pulled the plug in the bottom and shoved her out and she went down. Kids! They wanted to see the Titanic get bust. If they **were** *kids. I was under the impression that it was the lumber company, the timber operators up there, but I don't know, no way to tell.*

That's Rebecca L. Probably just before she went upstairs to go to bed. Her hair all down.

Very sexy. She's probably 15 or 16 there.

They were living down in the John Damon place.

What do you call the John Damon place?

Well, John Damon used to live there. Old John.

The following people participated in the making of this book: Gilbert Ward Tilton, Henry Bates Bridgham, Terry Brown, Jan Schreiber, Carol Shloss, Peter Werwath. Melissa Reed of the International Museum of Photography provided information about the camera used to take these pictures.

This book was printed at the Scroll Press in Danbury, Connecticut. The design is by Carol Shloss; the type, Linofilm Baskerville, was set by Wrightson Typographers; the paper is Mohawk Superfine. The edition was bound by A. Horowitz & Son.